A
Companion
to
Veritatis Splendor

A
Companion
to
Veritatis Splendor

Fr. James Tolhurst

First published in 1994

Gracewing
Fowler Wright Books
Southern Ave, Leominster
Herefordshire HR6 0QF

Gracewing Books are distributed

In New Zealand by
Catholic Supplies Ltd
80 Adelaide Rd
Wellington
New Zealand

In Australia by
Charles Paine Pty
8 Ferris Street
North Parramatta
NSW 2151 Australia

In Canada by
Meakin & Assoc.
Unit 17, 81, Auriga Drive
Nepean
Ontario KZE 7YS
Canada

In U.S.A. by
Morehouse Publishing
P.O. Box 1321
Harrisburg
PA 17105
U.S.A.

IMPRIMI POTEST
Paul Chavasse
STL Provost Cong Orat
11 March, 1994

NIHIL OBSTAT
Ieuan Wyn Jones,
Censor

IMPRIMATUR
John Aloysius Ward
OFM Cap,
Archbishop of Cardiff
28 March, 1994

The *Nihil Obstat* and *Imprimatur* are a declaration that a book or pamphlet is considered to be free from doctrinal or moral error. It is not implied that those who have granted the *Nihil Obstat* and *Imprimatur* agree with the contents, opinions or statements expressed.

Typesetting by Action Typesetting Limited, Gloucester
Printed by The Cromwell Press,
Broughton Gifford, Melksham, Wiltshire SN12 8PH

ISBN 085244 280 7

CONTENTS

PREFACE

LIVING THE TRUTH

More ink was spilled over *Veritatis Splendor* (The Splendour of Truth) before it saw the light of day than any other modern papal pronouncement. *After* its publication however it was greeted by an almost unanimous silence from the media, and by a surprising consensus from individuals who took the trouble to read it and openly admitted their appreciation of its contents.

It is addressed to all the bishops of the Catholic Church 'regarding certain fundamental questions of the Church's moral teaching'. Pope John Paul points out that this is the first time that these have been set out in detail (n. 115). Traditionally, moral theology has been divided into two areas: *fundamental* and *special*. The first area deals with the principles and the second, their particular application. *Veritatis Splendor* is seen as the first in a two-part treatment. Yet despite its theoretical character it is specifically designed to provide both a presentation of fundamental principles and an analysis of the many erroneous opinions relating to moral issues which have surfaced over the last few decades (n. 30). In an amazingly blunt sentence the Pope draws attention to the genuine crisis in the Church where 'it is no longer a matter of limited and occasional dissent, but of an overall and systematic calling into question of traditional moral doctrine' (n. 4).

It is Pope John Paul's intention therefore to present the fundamental principles of moral theology based upon Scripture and Tradition. He begins with the account of Jesus' meeting with the rich young man (Mt 19,16–23). It is no accident that he repeatedly returns to it throughout the encyclical.

The Pope highlights his seeking for what is good, and his encounter 'with One whom he calls Good. This leads on to a

1

discussion of the need to obey God who alone is good, and to acceptance of his Commandments which are the safeguard of human dignity. The Commandments are taken up by Christ, particularly in the Sermon of the Mount, which brings out their full meaning. The Beatitudes urge us to live by that perfect law which is the example of Christ himself.

The rich young man had indeed kept the commandments faithfully, but he wished to go further and Jesus invited him to that total self-giving which is the perfection of human freedom. This is not possible without the grace of God, but thanks to it, the gift of celibacy can be joyfully accepted (n. 22). Such *a living tradition* is part of the Church's responsibility, faithfully to interpret all the commands which Jesus gave to his apostles. This tradition is exemplified in the sacrifice of martyrs who have given their lives for such teaching, as well as in the preaching of the saints who have proclaimed it by their words and the purity of their lives. The Church is united not simply in faith, but also by its acceptance of the moral obligations of that faith: 'the unity of the Church is damaged not only by Christians who reject or distort the truths of faith, but also by those who disregard the moral obligations to which they are called by the Gospel' (n. 26).

In the second chapter of the document the Pope deals with various strands in moral theology which come into conflict with the Church's teaching: 'what is contrary to sound doctrine' (n. 30). He divides these into errors concerning the concept of freedom, the meaning of conscience and the fundamental option (cf. *Glossary*). Freedom, which is rightly perceived as the foundation of modern democracy, can be so exalted that it leads to a total arrogance where 'the individual conscience is accorded the status of a supreme tribunal of moral judgement which hands down categorical and infallible decisions about good and evil' (n. 32). But at the same time other moral theologians argue that man is so culturally and socially conditioned that almost the very existence and certainly the exercise of this freedom are called into question.

This leads on to a discussion of the natural law, which in some minds is thought to be a Catholic invention, rather than part of the great inherited tradition of jurisprudence. No Pope or Council, but Marcus Tullius Cicero stated 'There is in fact a true law – namely, right reason – which is in accordance with nature, applies to all men and is unchangeable and eternal'[1]. It is this universality and immutability (cf. n. 52f) which the Pope will return to in his discussion of the fundamental option.

Conscience, according to some theologians, can be reduced to a simple application of general moral norms to individual cases rather than that stern monitor, the voice of God, to which Cardinal Newman refers in his Letter to the Duke of Norfolk[2]. There should be no conflict between conscience and law, but rather conscience should confront man with the law of God in his heart.

The theology of the fundamental option, which dates from the 1960s, maintains that morality stems from a whole behaviour pattern, even if individual acts are immoral. This obviously calls into question the nature of mortal sin (n. 69f) which the Church has always taught deprives man of grace, and if he perseveres in it, of eternal happiness. The encyclical makes the point that a fundamental orientation can be changed radically by individual acts (n. 70).

When we come to consider the moral acts themselves, *Veritatis Splendor* again confronts the argument that intentions and motives can define the morality of actions. The encyclical rejects both *proportionalism* and *consequentialism* (cf. *Glossary*) because they do not take into account, that there can be an absolute prohibition of particular kinds of behaviour based on the objective malice of the object itself (n. 75f). It is precisely because the Church believes that there can be exceptionless moral norms that she also believes in mortal sin. It is largely because of the failure to accept such objective morality that various parties justify 'ethnic cleansing', genetic engineering, in-vitro fertilisation, sectarian killing, torture, or abortion. It is always possible to advocate loving motives or honourable causes or compassionate reasons, once we deny that there are certain actions that are always morally wrong.

When Pope John Paul preached at Wembley during his visit to the United Kingdom, he said 'The conflict between

[1] *De Republica* II. 33.

[2] Diff 2 pp. 247.250

certain values of the world and the values of the Gospel is an inescapable part of the Church's life, just as it is an inescapable part of the life of each one of us'[3]. This theme underlines the third chapter of *Veritatis Splendor* which calls for faith to be lived as a confession before God and mankind. Ultimately the total profession of faith in love can lead to martyrdom 'the outstanding sign of the holiness of the Church' and of the dignity of man created in God's image and likeness (n. 92f).

The Church does not flinch from defending the universal and unchanging moral norms, because without such a foundation there would be no freedom for anyone. In a ringing phrase the Pope reminds a world which has witnessed the downfall of the Soviet empire 'There is a risk of an alliance between democracy and ethical relativism, which would remove any sure moral reference point from political and social life. As history demonstrates, a democracy without values easily turns into open or thinly disguised totalitarianism' (n. 101). The world has need of a new evangelization which helps to restore the moral sense of objective truth and put forward the example of holiness which is its vindication.

Those who argue that such a presentation does not take account of human weakness are answered simply by the statement that the Church is as understanding as Christ was with sinners, but holds out to them the power of redemption and forgiveness. She is being faithful to her Master when she says that they must not make their weakness the criterion for morality and so lower the threshold, instead of levelling it up to the measure given by Christ of which Mary, Mother of Mercy is our pattern (cf. n.104. 118f).

Finally, the encyclical calls on moral theologians to set out the Church's moral teachings and give an example by loyally assenting to them (n. 110); and on bishops to exercise their pastoral concern in matters of moral teaching. This obviously has implications, as the Pope points out, in Catholic hospitals, counselling services, health-care facilities, and indeed, in schools and universities (n. 116). The Church must be seen to be consistent both in faith and in its practice of

[3] 29 May, 1982. *The Pope in Britain*. CTS 1982 p. 161

morality so that mankind can hear 'the voice of the truth about good and evil which is the voice of God who alone is good and who alone is love', (n. 117).

For this *Companion*, a detailed index to the text has been included as well as a glossary of some of the more difficult terms (in which I was ably assisted by Br. Philip Cleevely.) Perhaps the best way to understand these pages is to dwell on St Paul's concluding remarks in his letter to the Philippians: '... let your minds be filled with everything that is true, everything that is honourable, everything that is upright and pure, everything that we love and honour, and everything that can be thought virtuous or worthy of praise' (Phil 4,8).

James Tolhurst
Edgbaston, 1994

FREELY TO LIVE BY THE TRUTH

— an abridged version of the encyclical
Veritatis Splendor addressed to
the bishops of the Catholic Church
with index and glossary of terms
arranged by Fr James Tolhurst

VERITATIS SPLENDOR

INTRODUCTION

'Jesus Christ, the True Light which enlightens all who come into this world'

> *The splendour of truth* can be seen in all the works of creation but especially in man, created in the image and likeness of God (Gen 1,26).

1 It is through salvation in Jesus Christ, the true light that people become 'children of light' (Eph 5,8), and are made holy by obedience to the truth (I Pt 1,22).

Such obedience is not always easy because at the beginning man was led astray by the father of lies, Satan (cf. Jn 8,44), turning from God to exchange truth for a lie (Rom 1,25). But darkness and error can never take away Jn 18,38 the light of God and there remains always in man's heart that yearning for absolute truth and that search for meaning which spurs man on to that most painful of struggles in the depths of the heart and the conscience.

2 The most fundamental question put to man is *How do I distinguish good from evil*? This cannot be answered without the light of divine truth : 'What can bring us happiness?' many say. Lift up the light of your face on us, O Lord' (Ps 4,6). This light shines in all its beauty on Jesus Christ 'the reflection of God's glory' (Heb 1,3). The answer to mankind's questions must be sought in Him : 'It is only in

7

the mystery of the Word incarnate that light is shed on the mystery of man. For Adam, the first man, was a figure of the future man, namely, of Christ the Lord. It is Christ, the last Adam, who fully discloses man to himself and unfolds his noble calling by revealing the mystery of the Father and the Father's love'. Jesus casts the light of his truth on the Church so that it can be the light to the nations, offering to all the answer which comes from the Gospel, that must be preached to the ends of the earth (Mk 16,15). In every age she interprets the needs of each generation and responds with the light of the Gospel.   GS 22 · LG 1 · GS 4

3 The bishops of the Church in communion with the Pope, the successor of Peter, guide the faithful with their teaching, and address not only believers, but the whole of humanity, even those who do not know God, Christ or the Gospel. It is by following the path of the moral life that the way of salvation is open to all, for 'those who without any fault do not know anything about Christ or his Church, yet who search for God with a sincere heart and under the influence of grace, try to put into effect the will of God as known to them through the dictate of conscience ... can obtain eternal salvation ... Nor does divine Providence deny the helps that are necessary for salvation to those who, through no fault of their own have not yet attained to the express recognition of God, yet who strive, not without divine grace, to lead an upright life. For whatever goodness and truth is found in them is considered by the Church as a preparation for the Gospel and bestowed by Him who enlightens everyone that they may in the end have life.'   PP 13 · LG 16

The purpose of the present Encyclical

4 Over the years, but especially in the last two
centuries, the Popes, either individually or
together with the College of Bishops, have
spoken authoritatively about moral questions.
They have addressed the moral demands in the
areas of the family, human sexuality, social,
economic and political life.

Now it is necessary to reflect on the whole of
the Church's moral teaching in order to recall
certain fundamental truths which risk being
distorted or denied. The Church itself has been
affected by the spread of numerous doubts and
objections stemming from psychological,
cultural, social and theological critiques. In
addition traditional moral doctrine, has been
called into question by arguments based up on
ethical and anthropological presuppositions.
Behind all this lies a current of thought which
exalts human freedom and detaches it from its
essential relationship to truth. Thus the
universal and permanent validity of the natural
law is rejected, the Church's moral teachings
are deemed 'unacceptable' and individuals are
held to be free to make up their own minds,
listening simply to exhortations from the
Church which puts forward certain values that
they presume themselves free to consider.

There is also a lack of harmony present in
seminaries and theological faculties between
the traditional dogmas of the Church and
certain theological positions. This divergence
relates to the ways in which the commandments apply and, are binding in the daily
decisions of individuals and societies in all
circumstances. Also whether communion with
the Church can prescind from moral
behaviour and the decisions of the individual
conscience and depend on faith alone.

5 In the light of all this, I came to the decision –
as I announced in my Apostolic Letter, *Spiritus
Domini*, issued on 1 August 1987 on the second
centenary of the death of St Alphonsus Maria
de' Liguori – to write an Encyclical to treat
'more fully and more deeply the issues
regarding the very foundations of moral
theology'. Foundations which are being
undermined by certain present-day tendencies.
I address myself to you, Venerable Brothers in
the Episcopate who share with me the responsibility of safeguarding sound teaching (2 Tim
4,3), with the intention of clearly setting forth
certain aspects of doctrine which are of crucial
importance in facing what is certainly a
genuine crisis with serious implications for the
moral life of the faithful with all that implies.

The reason for the delay is that it seemed
fitting to allow the *Catechism of the Catholic
Church* (which contains a systematic
exposition of moral teaching) to be published
first. The Catechism is a sure and authentic
reference text for teaching Catholic doctrine FD 4
on the whole of the moral life of the children
of God. This Encyclical will limit itself to
dealing with certain fundamental questions of
the Church's moral teaching with particular
reference to the issues being debated by moral
theologians and raised in relation to ethical
questions. The purpose of the Encyclical is to
set forth, with regard to the problems being
discussed, the principles of a moral teaching
based upon Sacred Scripture and the living
Apostolic Tradition. At the same time it is
intended to cast light on the presuppositions
and consequences of the dissent surrounding
that teaching.   DV 10

CHAPTER ONE

'TEACHER WHAT GOOD MUST I DO?

Christ and the answer to the question about morality

6 We are told in the account of the rich young
man (Mt 19,16f) that he asked Jesus
"'Teacher, what good must I do to have
eternal life?' And he said to him, 'Why do you
ask me about what is good? There is only one
who is good. If you would enter life, keep the
commandments.' He said to him, 'Which?'
And Jesus said, 'You shall not kill; You shall
not commit adultery; You shall not steal; You
shall not bear false witness; Honour your
father and your mother; and, You shall love
your neighbour as yourself'. The young man
said to him, 'I have kept all these; what do I
still lack?' Jesus said to him, 'If you would be
perfect, go, sell what you possess and give to
the poor, and you will have treasure in heaven;
and come, follow me.'" (Mt 19,16–21).

7 The young man in the Gospel allows us to
recognise the desires of the human heart
appealing to the absolute Good which attracts
and encourages us. God willed his Church so
that all might find Christ and Christ might
walk with each person the path of life. The RH 13
Second Vatican Council, for this reason called
for a renewal of moral theology so that its
teaching could make this clear. OT 16

11

'Teacher, what good must I do to have eternal life?'

8 The young man senses instinctively that there
is a connection between moral good and the
fulfilment of his own destiny. Since he is a
devout Israelite (Mt 19,20), he is not ignorant
of the answers which the Law gives, but
prompted undoubtedly by the attractiveness
of the person of Jesus he feels the need to ask
further about what is morally good.

People today need to turn to the same Jesus
Christ, the Teacher, who is always present in
the Church, to open up the Scriptures and
fully reveal the will of the Father. Because he
is the Alpha and the Omega of human history,
(Rev 1,8;21,6;22,13) he alone can reveal to us
the heart of our vocation and the true reality
of our inner selves.   RH 10

9 **'There is only one who is good'**

Before he answers his question, Jesus wants
the young man to reflect that 'goodness of
life' can only be found by turning one's mind
and heart to the 'One who alone is good' (cf.
Mk 10,18;Lk 18,19). To ask about good
ultimately means to turn towards God, the
fullness of goodness – the goodness that
attracts and at the same time obliges man, has
its source in God, and indeed is God himself.
He is the source of man's true happiness and
the final end of all human activity.

10 What man is, and what he must do, becomes
clear as soon as God reveals himself. In the
'ten words' of the Covenant which we know as
The Commandments, the Lord who brought
Israel out of the land of Egypt makes himself
known and acknowledged as the One who
'alone is good'. In spite of man's sins he
remains faithful to his love for man and gives

him his Law (cf. Ex 19,9–24; 20,18–21) in order to restore man's original peace and harmony with the Creator and with his creation, so that man may be drawn into his divine love (Lev 26,12).

The moral life is the response due to the many free initiatives taken by God out of love for man (cf. Dt 6,4–7). As St Leo says 'For the one who loves God it is enough to be pleasing to the One whom he loves; for no greater reward should be sought than that love itself; charity in fact is of God in such a way that God himself is charity'. Sermon 92 ch.3 PL 54,454

11 The one who is good reminds us of the 'first tablet' of the Commandments which calls us to acknowledge God as the one Lord of all. The *good* involves belonging to God, obeying him, walking humbly with him, with justice and loving kindness (cf. Mic 6,8). This acknowledgement of the Lord as God is the very heart of the Law, from which the particular precepts flow, and to which they are themselves ordered.

But if God alone is the Good and all Holy (cf. Is 6,3) it is impossible for man to 'fulfil' the Law even if he is strenuous in its observance. Such 'fulfilment' can only come from a gift of God. This is finally revealed to the young man by Jesus himself in the invitation: 'Come, follow me' (Mt 19,21).

12 **'If you wish to enter into life, keep The Commandments'**

God has already given the answer to the question about the good, by the innate gift which man possesses in his own nature, known as the natural law, by which he understands what good must be done and what evil must be avoided. But he also provides the answer in the history of Israel and in particular the 'ten words' or Commandments of Sinai by which the people of Israel were brought into existence (cf. Ex 24) as his own possession and a holy nation (Ex 19,5–6). The gift of the Commandments (or Decalogue) was a promise and sign of the new and definitive covenant which would be written not on stone, but on the human heart (Jer 31,31–34; Ez 36,24–28). Jesus makes the connection between eternal life ('If you wish to enter into life') and obedience to God's commandments, because they show man the path of life and they lead to it. Jesus, as the new Moses once again gives man The Commandments. He confirms them and proposes them as the way and the condition to salvation. The Commandments in the Old Covenant were linked to the promise of the possession of the land where the people would live in freedom and righteousness (cf. Dt 6,20–25). In the New Covenant Jesus declares from another Mountain that he promises the Kingdom of Heaven (cf. Mt 5–7). In life this means the possession of the light of truth, a source of meaning and a share in the full following of Christ, and after death, its perfection as a participation in the very life of God. After speaking to the rich young man Jesus tells his disciples 'Every one who has left houses or brothers or sisters or father or mother or children or lands, for my name's sake, will receive a hundredfold, [in this time: Lk 18,30] and inherit eternal life' (Mt 19,29).

13 Jesus' answer is not enough for the young man who asks, which of the commandments must be kept (Mt 19,18) to show that he acknowledges God's holiness. Jesus replies by drawing attention to the central importance that the

commandments must hold with regard to every other precept. But he singles out those which belong to the 'second tablet' of the Decalogue, which are summed up in the commandment of love of neighbour.

The commandments of which Jesus reminds the young man are meant to safeguard the singular dignity of the individual 'the only creature that God has wanted for its own sake', GS 24 by protecting his life, his communion in marriage, his property, his reputation. The commandments thus represent the basic condition for love of neighbour as well as being the proof of that love. They are also the first necessary step on the journey towards freedom. 'The beginning of freedom' says St Augustine 'is to be free from crimes ... such as murder, adultery, fornication, theft, fraud, sacrilege and so forth. When one is without these crimes (and every Christian should be without them), one begins to lift up one's head In towards freedom. But this is only the beginning Iohannis of freedom, not perfect freedom ...' Tr 41,10

14 This does not imply that love of neighbour is being put higher, or even set apart from love of God. This is made clear in the conversation between Jesus and the teacher of the Law who also asked him what he should do to inherit eternal life (Lk 10,25). Jesus refers to the two commandments of love of God and love of neighbour saying that observing these will answer his question. But it is significant that the teacher then asks 'And who is my neighbour?' (Lk 10,29) which elicits from Jesus the parable of the Good Samaritan (Lk 10,30−37). This still remains a vital key to understanding the commandment of love of neighbour.

Both commandments are inseparably connected. The life and death of Jesus himself is both a sign of love of the Father and of love for humanity (cf. Jn 13,1). Without love for one's brother it is not possible to have love for God (1 Jn 4,20; Mt 25,31–46).

15 In Jesus, the Scriptures reach their fulfilment because they bear witness to him (Mt 5,17;Jn 5,39). He also is that living and eternal link between the Old and New Covenants and the fullness of the Law because he came not to abolish it, but to bring it to fulfilment by interiorising the demands of the Law and bringing out its fullest meaning. The Commandments must not be understood as a minimum limit not to be surpassed, but rather as that path towards perfection. Thus the commandment 'You shall not kill' becomes a call to an attentive love which protects and promotes the life of one's neighbour. The precept prohibiting adultery becomes an invitation to purity in relationships (cf. Mt 5,21f). Jesus by his fulfilment of the Law becomes a living and personal Law, inviting all to follow him, and giving through the Holy Spirit, the grace and strength to bear witness to that Law of Christ in personal choices and actions (cf. Jn 13,34–35).

16 **'If you wish to be perfect'** (Mt 19,21)

The young man asks Jesus a further question: 'I have kept all these [Commandments] what do I still lack?' (Mt 19,20) It is not easy to say 'I have kept all these' with a clear conscience if one has any understanding of the real meaning of the demands contained in God's Law. Yet even with a generous fulfilment of the legal observances the young man, face to face with Jesus, realises that he is still lacking something.

The Good Teacher in his turn conscious of his yearning, leads him to that greater gift of oneself : 'If you would be perfect, go, sell what you possess and give to the poor, and you will have treasures in heaven; and come, follow me' (Mt 19,21).

Jesus' answers must be seen in the context of his Sermon on the Mount, in particular the Beatitudes (Mt 5,3–12) The first of these concerns the *poor* in spirit (Mt 5,3). Every beatitude promises, from a particular viewpoint that very 'good' which is the opening on to eternal life and its anticipation here on earth. As they are a sort of self-portrait of Christ himself, so they are invitations to CC discipleship and communion with him. 1717

17 The response to Jesus' invitation requires a commitment to respect the demands of the Commandments, but it also requires the grace of God which makes possible that free and mature gift of self. The follower of Christ knows that his vocation is to freedom (cf. Gal 5,13) and such freedom is not in opposition to God's Law although unfortunately we can 'use our freedom as an opportunity for the flesh' (Gal 5,3). St Augustine, speaking of the observance of the Commandments as a kind of incipient, imperfect freedom says: 'Why, someone will ask, is it not yet perfect? Because "I see in my members another law at war with the law of my reason" . . . In part freedom, in part slavery: not yet complete freedom, not yet pure, not yet whole, because we are not yet in eternity. In part we retain our weakness and in part we have attained freedom. All our sins were destroyed in Baptism, but does it follow that no weakness remained after iniquity was destroyed? Had none remained, we would live without sin in this life. But who would dare to

say this except someone who is proud,
someone unworthy of the mercy of our
deliverer?... Therefore, since some weakness
has remained in us, I dare to say that to the
extent to which we serve God we are free, In
while to the extent that we follow the law of Iohannis
sin, we are still slaves.'   Tr 41,10

18 Those who live by the 'flesh' experience God's
    law as a burden which denies or restricts their
    freedom. But those who 'walk by the Spirit'
    (Gal 5,16) find in God's Law the way in which
    they are enabled to practise love as something
    freely chosen. They are also prompted by
    God's grace to that full freedom of the
    children of God (cf. Rom 8,21), which seeks to
    live the Commandments in their fullness,
    tending towards that perfection whose
    measure is God alone (cf. Mt 5,48;Lk 6,36).

'Come, follow me' (Mt 19,21)

19 Jesus who invites the young man to give up his
    wealth and indeed his very self, calls all people
    to follow him. As the people of Israel followed
    God through the desert to the Promised Land
    (cf. Ex 13,21), so every disciple drawn by the
    Father must follow Jesus (cf. Jn 6,44); not
    simply hearing his teaching and obeying his
    words, but also sharing his life and his free
    and loving obedience to his Father's will. He is
    the light of the world and the light of life (Jn
    8,12), the good shepherd who leads his sheep
    to pasture, the way, the truth and the life (cf
    Jn 10,11–16;14,6).

20 This following of Christ (*sequela Christi*)
    requires an imitation of him in his way of
    acting, his words, his deeds and his love for
    the brethren out of love for God : 'This is my

commandment, that you love one another as I have loved you ... By this all men will know that you are my disciples' (Jn 15,12;13,35). The invitation given to the young man asks him to imitate the very love of the 'Good' Teacher who loved his own 'to the end', even to the Cross (Jn 13,1; Mt 16,24).

21 This is not possible except by grace, and the disciple is conformed to Christ by the active presence of the Holy Spirit in the depths of his being. Through Baptism he is clothed with Christ (cf. Gal 3,27) and so able to be led by the Spirit and manifest the fruits of that same Spirit in his life (Gal 5,16–25). The Eucharist, the source of eternal life is the source and power of that complete gift of self and his assimilation to Christ (cf. Jn 6,51–58).

22 **'With God all things are possible'** (Mt 19,26)

We are told that the young man went away sorrowful 'for he had great possessions' (Mt 19,22). But not only the rich man, but also the disciples are taken aback by Jesus' call to perfection: 'They were greatly astounded and said, 'Then who can be saved?' (Mt 19,25). Jesus replies 'With men this is impossible, but with God all things are possible' (Mt 19,26).

Jesus gives a similar reply to the Pharisees who ask him about the Mosaic Law on marriage, which allowed divorce. Jesus in rejecting this right, appeals to God's original plan for mankind (Mt 19,8). The disciples remark 'If such is the case of a man with his wife, it is not expedient to marry' (Mt 19,10). Jesus replies that the charism of celibacy 'for the Kingdom of Heaven' is not possible without the gift of God's grace, 'Not everyone can accept this saying, but only those to whom it is given' (Mt 19,11).

As the Lord receives the love of his Father, so he communicates that love to his disciples which makes them capable of making that perfect response to Christ's invitation (Jn 15,9). St Augustine asks: 'Does love bring about the keeping of the Commandments, or does the keeping of the Commandments bring about love?... Who can doubt that love comes first? For the one who does not love has no reason for keeping the commandments'. In Iohannis Tr 82,3

23 The function of the (Old) Law according to St Paul enabled sinful man to recognise his powerlessness and prepared him to ask for and receive the Spirit of life in Christ Jesus, setting us free to carry out God's Commandments (cf. Rom 8,2) 'The Law was given that grace might be sought', says St Augustine; 'and grace was given, that the law might be fulfilled'. Living the life of God is only possible as a result of divine grace which heals, restores and transforms the human heart: 'for the Law was given through Moses; grace and truth came through Jesus Christ' (Jn 1,17). De Spiritu et Littera 19,34

24 It is this awareness of having received the gift of the love of God which generates and sustains our free response which St Augustine has expressed in his prayer *Da quod iubes et iube quod vis* (Grant what you command and command what you will). God's gift does not lessen, but rather reinforces the moral demands of love: 'This is his commandment, that we should believe in the name of his Son Jesus Christ and love one another just as he has commanded us' (1 Jn 3,32). St Thomas, summing up the teaching of the Fathers can say 'The New Law is the grace of the Holy Confessions 10,29,40

Spirit given through faith in Christ'. The New
Law is not content simply to say what must be
done, but gives the power to 'do what is true'
(cf. Jn 3,21). St John Chrysostom says that it
was promulgated at the descent of the Holy
Spirit on the day of Pentecost, and that the
apostles 'did not come down from the mountain carrying, like Moses, tablets of stone in
their hands; but they came down carrying the
Holy Spirit in their hearts ... having become
by his grace a living Law, a living book.'

ST I–II
Q 106 a.1
and ad 2

In
Matthaeum
Hom.1,1
PG 57,15

'Lo, I am with you always, to the consummation of the world' (Mt 28,20)

25 Jesus' conversation with the young man continues in every period of history including our
own. Christ alone is capable of giving a full and
definitive answer to the question 'What good
must I do to possess eternal life?' He is always
present in our midst as he promised (Mt 28,20)
in his Body which is the Church. He has given
to his disciples and their successors the Holy
Spirit who brings to their remembrance and
teaches them to understand all that he
commanded them (cf. Jn 14,26; Mt 28,20).
These moral prescriptions must be faithfully
kept and continually put into practice in the
various cultures through the course of history.

26 From the beginning, the apostles, by virtue of
their pastoral responsibility to preach the
Gospel did not simply issue exhortations and
directions concerned with particular historical
and cultural situations, but also had a pastoral
care for the conduct of believers as they were
concerned for the purity of the faith and the
conduct of the Sacraments (cf. Rom 12–15; 1
Cor 11–14; Gal 5–6; Eph 4–6; Col 3–4; 1 Pt
and Jas).

Irenaeus
AH IV
26,2–5

Justin
Apologia
1,66
PG
6,427–430

No damage must be done to the harmony
between faith and life: the unity of the Church
is damaged not only by Christians who reject   Ign Ant
or distort the truths of faith, but also by those   Ad
who disregard the moral obligations to which   Magnesios
they are called by the Gospel (cf I Cor 5,9 – 13).   VI, 1–2

27   The Church continues to preserve the faith and
moral life by that *living Tradition* which comes
from the apostles and develops under the   DV 8
assistance of the Holy Spirit. She professes by
the lips of her Fathers and Doctors the truth of
the Incarnate Word, and puts his commands
and his love into practice in the lives of her
Saints and in the sacrifice of her Martyrs.

The *authentic interpretation* of the Law also
develops with the help of the Holy Spirit, who
being the source of Jesus' commandments is
also the guarantee that they will be reverently
preserved, faithfully expounded and correctly
applied. This task is committed to those
charged with the Church's living Magisterium,
whose authority is exercised in the name of
Jesus Christ. The Church is thus revealed as the
'pillar and foundation of the truth' (1 Tim   LG 10
3,15), including the truth concerning moral
action. Indeed 'the Church has the right always
and everywhere to proclaim moral principles,
even in respect of the social order, and to make
judgements about any human matter in so far
as this is required by fundamental human
rights or the salvation of souls.' The   CIC 747
Magisterium of the Church in fidelity to Jesus
Christ and in continuity with the Church's
tradition, senses the duty of offering its
discernment and teaching on the questions
frequently debated in moral theology in the
context of the new tendencies and theories
which are now current, so that man may
journey towards truth and freedom.

CHAPTER TWO

'DO NOT BE CONFORMED TO THIS WORLD'
(Rom 12,2)

The church and the discernment of certain tendencies in contemporary moral theology

'Teaching what befits sound doctrine' (Tit 2:1)

28 Our meditation on the dialogue between Jesus and the rich young man has brought together the essential teaching of Revelation with regard to moral action: the subordination of man and his activity to God, who alone is good; the relationship between the moral good of human acts and eternal life; Christian discipleship with its perspective of perfect love and the gift of the Holy Spirit, source and means of the moral life in the 'new creation' (cf. 2 Cor 5,17).

    The Church has achieved a doctrinal development with regard to moral principles as well as the truths of faith which must be believed.   GS 22

29 This is linked to the science called 'moral theology' which is concerned with morality : the good and evil of human acts and of the person who performs them, acknowledging the origin and end of moral action is found in God, who alone is good.

    Vatican II invited scholars to take 'special care for the renewal of moral theology', in such a way that 'its scientific presentation, increasingly based on the teaching of Scripture, will cast light on the exalted vocation of the faithful in Christ and on their obligation to bear fruit in charity for the life of the world'. The Council also encouraged OT 16 theologians, 'while respecting the methods and requirements of theological science, to look for a more appropriate way of communicating doctrine to the people of their time; since there is a difference between the deposit or the truths of faith and the manner in which they are expressed, keeping the same meaning and the same judgement.' The GS 62 Church, and in particular the Bishops, who are entrusted with teaching the faith, are appreciative of the work of theologians and encourage them in their research inspired with that profound and authentic 'fear of the Lord, which is the beginning of wisdom' (Prov 1,7).

30 But there are certain interpretations of Christian morality which are not consistent with 'sound teaching' (cf. 2 Tim 4,3). It is my intention in this Encyclical to state the principles necessary for discerning what is contrary to 'sound doctrine', while drawing attention to aspects of the Church's moral teaching which appear exposed to error, ambiguity or neglect. Such questions as: what is freedom and what is its relationship to the truth contained in God's law? what is the role of conscience in human moral development? how do we determine the specific rights and duties of the human person, using the criterion of The Good? These are all summed up in the question put by the rich young man 'Teacher, what good must I do to have eternal life?'

'You will know the truth, and the truth will make you free' (Jn 8,32)

31 Contemporary debates on morality are all closely related to the crucial issue of human freedom. Today people demand that they be allowed to 'enjoy the use of their own responsible judgement and freedom, and decide on their actions on grounds of duty and conscience, without external pressure or coercion.' The right to religious freedom and DH 1 respect for conscience is seen as the foundation for individual human rights. But this RH 17 authentic insight (which is one of the positive achievements of modern culture) can be separated from the concept of man as created in the image of God, and so distorted.   GS 11

32 Certain interpretations exalt freedom to such an extent that it becomes an absolute value and the conscience the supreme tribunal of moral judgement. In such a case the claims of truth disappear and its place is taken by sincerity, authenticity, 'being at peace with oneself': essentially subjective criteria. This is not unconnected with a loss of the idea of universal truth which can be known by human reason. Once this idea has gone conscience is no longer seen as an act of the mind which applies the universal knowledge of good in a specific situation but instead gives the conscience the right to determine its own criteria of good and evil. This is very congenial to an individualistic ethic which turns its back on the concept of human nature.

33 But in contrast with this, the behavioural science school which has drawn attention to the psychological and social conditioning which affects the exercise of human freedom

and have in some cases gone on to question or
deny the ability to act with true freedom.

Behaviourists who in fact misuse scientific
research about the human person, can argue
from customs, behaviour patterns and the
existence of human institutions to a denial of
human values; with a consequent relativistic
concept of morality.

34 The answer that Christ gave to the young man
cannot prescind from the issue of human
freedom because only when he is free can man
turn to what is good. Vatican II, which notes
that many of our contemporaries who regard
freedom highly often cultivate it as a licence to
do anything they please, speaks of 'genuine
freedom'. It says that this is 'an outstanding
manifestation of the divine image in man. For
God willed to leave man 'in the power of his
own counsel' (Sir 15,14), so that he would seek
his Creator of his own accord and would
freely arrive at full and blessed perfection by
cleaving to God'. Every individual has a right   GS 17
to be respected in his search for the truth, but
there is a grave prior obligation to seek the
truth and to adhere to it when it is found. As
Cardinal John Henry Newman, that outstanding defender of the rights of conscience
forcefully put it: 'Conscience has rights   Diff 2
because it has duties'.   p.250

Certain interpretations, under the influence
of subjectivist and individualistic currents of
thought analyse the relationship of freedom to
the moral law in such a way as to undermine
the dependence of freedom on truth which has
found so authoritative expression in the words
of Christ: 'You will know the truth, and the
truth will make you free'.

I. Freedom and Law

35 *'Of the tree of the knowledge of good and evil you shall not eat'* (Gen 2,17)

In the Book of Genesis we read that 'The Lord God commanded the man, saying, "You may eat freely of every tree of the garden; but of the tree of the knowledge of good and evil you shall not eat, for in the day that you eat of it you shall die"' (Gen 2,16–17). Man is, in other words, free to understand and accept God's commands and can eat 'of every tree of the garden'. But that freedom is not unlimited. The power to decide what is good and evil does not belong to man, but to God alone. Man is called to accept the moral law given by God, and his freedom finds its fulfilment in the acceptance of that law because God, who alone is good, knows what is good for man and by virtue of his love proposes this good to man in his Law. God's law does not reduce or do away with human freedom but rather promotes and protects it.

Those who allege a conflict between freedom and law often proceed to break the link between them. This would in fact make truth itself a creation of freedom (if freedom were allowed to establish its own values and enjoy absolute sovereignty).

36 Catholic moral theology, while never attempting to set human freedom against the divine law has carried out a re-examination of the role of reason and faith in identifying moral norms. This has taken into consideration the behavioural sciences, inter-personal relationships and the relation between man and his environment.

But there have been people who have disregarded the present state of fallen nature and the need for Revelation, and have proposed a merely 'human' morality which man in an autonomous manner lays down for himself. This denies that the natural moral law has God as its author and that man, by the use of reason, participates in the eternal law, which it is not for him to establish.

HG AAS 42 p.561 – 2

37 Certain moral theologians have introduced a distinction between an ethical order, human in origin, and an order of salvation regarding God and one's neighbour. This is in effect a denial that Revelation contains any specific moral content which is universally and permanently valid. They would reduce the word of God to an exhortation and would deny that the Magisterium had any competency in moral matters. This is incompatible with Catholic teaching.

Trent DS 1569 – 1571

'God left man in the power of his own counsel' (Sir 15,14)

38 Vatican II comments : 'God willed to leave men in the power of his own counsel, so that he would seek his Creator of his own accord and would freely arrive at full and blessed perfection by cleaving to God.' These words tell us how man shares in God's dominion by having a certain dominion over himself. St Gregory of Nyssa describes this in terms of kingship: 'The soul shows its royal and exalted character ... in that it is free and self-governed, swayed autonomously by its own will. Of whom else can this be said, save a king? ... Thus human nature, created to rule other creatures, was by its likeness to the King of the universe made as it were a living image, partaking with the

GS 17

De Hominis Opificio 4 PG 44, 135 – 6

Archetype both in dignity and in name.'

This dominion is exercised over the world in which he lives in accordance with the command of the Creator 'Fill the earth and subdue it' (Gen 1,28). It consists in discovering and utilizing the laws which are written into the environment. GS 36

39 But man himself has been entrusted to his own care and responsibility so that he can seek his Creator and attain perfection through performing morally good acts. If man prescinds from his Creator then this will have a disastrous impact on the earth and on man himself. GS 36

40 The Council refers to the role of human reason in discovering and applying the moral law. Reason draws its own truth and authority from the eternal law, which is none other than divine wisdom itself. The moral law by virtue of natural human reason becomes a properly human law. Indeed, the natural law 'is nothing other than the light of understanding infused in us by God, by which we grasp what must be done and what must be avoided. God gave this light and this law to man in creating him'. Man therefore possesses in himself his own law, but not independently of the Creator and Lawgiver: 'But of the tree of the knowledge of good and evil you shall not eat, for in the day that you eat of it you shall die' (Gen 2,17). Aquinas Duo Praec Prolog.

41 Man's genuine personal moral freedom and God's law meet and are called to intersect in the sense that man freely obeys God and God freely creates. Obedience is not therefore to something extraneous to man himself and intolerant of his freedom, because this would mean a form of alienation contrary to Revelation and the dignity of the human person as well as to divine wisdom made incarnate in Christ.

Others speak not of autonomy but rather of a participated *theonomy* since human reason and human will share in God's wisdom and providence. By forbidding man to eat of the tree, God makes clear that man does not possess such 'knowledge' as his own, but only participates in it. Law must therefore be considered an expression of divine wisdom: by submitting to the law, freedom submits to the truth of creation.

'Blessed is the man who takes delight in the law of the Lord' (Ps 1,1–2)

42 Man's freedom, patterned on God's freedom relies on obedience to the divine law in order to live up to one's human dignity and to abide in the truth: 'Human dignity requires man to act through conscious and free choice, as motivated and prompted personally from within, and not through blind internal impulse or merely external pressure. Man achieves such dignity when he frees himself from all subservience to his feelings, and in a free choice of the good, pursues his own end by effectively and assiduously marshalling the appropriate means.'   GS 17

In his journey towards God, the One who 'alone is good' man must freely choose to do good and avoid evil, using the light of natural reason. But this light of natural reason is nothing other than an imprint on us of the divine light: 'Who will make us see good? The light of your face, Lord, is signed upon us' (Ps 4,6 Vulgate). This discernment between good and evil is the function of the *natural* law, which is called natural, because it is proper to human nature.   Aquinas ST I–II Q91 a.2

CC 1955

43 Vatican II refers back to the classic teaching on God's eternal law: '(The) supreme rule of life is the divine law itself, the eternal, objective and universal law by which God out of his wisdom and love arranges, directs and governs the whole world and the paths of the human community. God has enabled man to share in this divine law, and hence man is able under the gentle guidance of God's providence increasingly to recognize the unchanging truth'. St Augustine defines this as 'the reason or the will of God, who commands us to respect the natural order and forbids us to disturb it'. St Thomas talks of 'the type of the divine wisdom moving all things to their due end'. God cares for man through a providential concern which works through reason in the case of humanity, calling man to share in his own guidance of the world. The natural law is thus the human expression of God's eternal law.

DH 3

Contra Faust 22 c.27 PL 42,418

ST I–II 93 a.1

44 The Church has often referred to the Thomistic doctrine of natural law. Leo XIII emphasized the essential subordination of reason and human law to the Wisdom of God and his law: 'this prescription of human reason could not have the force of law unless it were the voice and interpreter of some higher reason to which our spirit and our freedom must be subject ... All of this, clearly, could not exist in man if, as his own supreme legislator, he gave himself the rule of his own actions.'

Libertas Praestant. Acta VIII Romae 1889 p.219.

This discernment between good and evil is made possible in particular by the help that divine revelation gives to human reason, especially through the law which God gave to the Chosen People. Israel was called to obey The Commandments as a sign of election and

of God's covenant with them: 'What great
nation is there that has a god so near to it as
the Lord our God is to us, whenever we call
upon him? And what great nation is there that
has statutes and ordinances so righteous as all
this law which I set before you this day? ...
Blessed is the man who walks not in the
counsel of the wicked, nor stands in the way of
sinners, nor sits in the seat of scoffers, but his
delight is in the law of the Lord and on his law
he meditates day and night ... The law of the
Lord is perfect, reviving the soul: the
testimony of the Lord is sure, making wise the
simple; the precepts of the Lord are right,
rejoicing the heart; the commandment of the
Lord is pure, enlightening the eyes.' (Dt
4,7–8; Ps 1,1–2; 19,8–9).

45 The Church accepts this gift of the law which is
authentically interpreted and fulfilled in the
light of the Gospel, 'the law of the Spirit of life
in Christ Jesus' (Rom 8,2). St Thomas writes
that this law 'can be called law in two ways.
First the law of the spirit is the Holy Spirit ...
who, dwelling in the soul, not only teaches
what it is necessary to do by enlightening the
intellect on the things to be done, but also
inclines the affections to act with upright-
ness ... Second, the law of the spirit can be
called the proper effect of the Holy Spirit, and
thus faith working through love (Gal 5,6),
which teaches inwardly about the things to be
done ... and inclines the affections to act'.

cf Jer
31,31–33
2 Cor 3,3
17.

In Epist.
ad Rom
c8 lect.1

'What the law requires is written on their hearts' (Rom 2,15)

46 The alleged conflict between freedom and law
re-emerges in our own time with regard to the
natural law and to nature itself. Such debates

raged during the Council of Trent. Previous DS 1521 ages have seen man being subject to the unbreakable laws of 'nature', and today this takes the form of a subjection to psychological processes and behaviour patterns. Some *ethicists* argue from statistical surveys and opinion polls to support their position. Other *moralists*, regard freedom as in conflict or in opposition to nature. Nature is understood by some to be the raw material for human action which needs to be overcome by freedom, because it is a limiting factor. For others human nature is reduced to a readily available biological and social material: the human body, its make-up and its processes and indeed, everything found in the world apart from freedom. But this means that man does not have a nature and would be nothing more than his own freedom.

47 Other people object that the Church presents what are in effect biological laws, as moral laws which have a permanent and unchanging character with universally valid norms. The condemnation of contraception, direct sterilization, autoeroticism, pre-marital sexual relations, artificial insemination and homosexual relations was, it is argued, based on such a naturalistic conception of morality. It is further argued that such a negative evaluation fails to take into consideration man's character as a rational, free being and ignores his cultural conditioning, because man must freely determine the meaning of his own behaviour.

48 In this theory a freedom claiming to be absolute, treats the human body as a raw datum and a presupposition for the free choice to be made by the person, and extrinsic

to him or her. There would be no question of human nature or the body being a reference point for moral decisions because we are in the realm of the 'physical' or the 'pre-moral'. The tension between freedom and nature considered in this reductive way is resolved by assuming a division within man himself.

Such a theory contradicts the Church's teachings on the unity of the human person, who is one unity because of the spiritual and immortal soul that is its form. The definitions of the Councils of Vienne and Lateran V are DS 902, not only concerned with the resurrection of 1440 the body, but also with the unity of reason and free will with the bodily and sense faculties. It is in the unity of body and soul that the person is the subject of his own moral acts. Since the human person cannot be reduced to a freedom that dictates its own parameters, the moral requirements imply respect for certain fundamental goods if one would not fall into relativism.

49 A doctrine which dissociates the moral act from its actual bodily expression is contrary to the teaching of Scripture and Tradition. Such a doctrine misunderstands the meaning of the body and its behaviour and reduces the human person to a purely formal freedom. St Paul declares immoral 'idolaters, adulterers, sexual perverts, thieves, gluttons, drunkards, revilers and robbers' saying that they are excluded from the Kingdom of God (1 Cor 6,9). The Council of Trent which repeats this condemnation lists as 'mortal sins' or 'immoral practices' certain specific kinds of behaviour because body and soul are inseparable; they stand or fall together.

50 Natural law therefore refers to the nature of the human person, in the unity of his spiritual and biological inclinations and of all the other specific characteristics which go up to make a human being. The natural moral law GS 51 'expresses and lays down the purposes, rights and duties which are based upon the bodily and spiritual nature of the human person. Therefore this law cannot be thought of as simply a set of norms on the biological level; rather it must be defined as the rational order whereby man is called by the Creator to direct and regulate his life and actions and in particular to make used of his own body.' DVi iii Thus the foundation of the absolute respect for human life is to be found in the dignity of the person and not simply in the natural inclination of self-preservation. There is no division between freedom and nature because these are harmoniously bound together and interlinked.

51 **'From the beginning it was not so'** (Mt 19,8)

The alleged conflict between freedom, and nature also has an impact on the universal and unchanging nature of the natural law. The separation which some postulate between the freedom of individuals and the nature which all have in common, obscures the perception of the universality of the moral law on the part of reason. But inasmuch as the natural law expresses the dignity of the human person and lays the foundation for his fundamental rights and duties, it guarantees the uniqueness of each person and builds up the true communion of persons. Col 3,14

52 There are certain unchanging precepts which are universally valid, such as the worship of God and honouring one's parents. These unite

in the same common good all people of every   GS 10
period of history, created for the 'same divine   PH 4
calling and destiny'. Such precepts are applied   GS 29
to particular acts through the judgement of
conscience. The acting subject makes the truth
contained in the law his own by his acts and
virtues. This also applies to the negative
precepts which forbid a course of action
always, without exception (*semper et pro
semper*). This does not mean that prohibitions
are more important than positive commandments, but the love of God and neighbour
which does not have any upper limit, does
have a level below which the commandment is
broken. In addition there are kinds of
behaviour which can never, in any situation be
allowed; even if someone may be hindered
from doing a good act, he cannot be stopped
from refusing to commit an evil one, to the
extent of martyrdom if necessary. Jesus
affirms that these prohibitions admit no
exceptions : 'If you wish to enter into life,
keep the commandments ... You shall not
murder, You shall not commit adultery, You
shall not steal, You shall not bear false
witness'. (Mt 19,17–18).

53 There are contemporaries who call the immutability of the natural law into question
and with it, the existence of objective norms of   GS 16
morality; which are valid for all time, past,
present and future. They ask whether it is
possible to make such a determination when
the future course of humanity is unknown?
    Although man always exists in a particular
changing culture he is not totally defined by it.
The progress of cultures demonstrates that
there is something in man which transcends
culture and that this is the human nature he
possesses. It would also render meaningless

Jesus' reference to the 'beginning' (cf. Mt
19,1−9), so 'the Church affirms that
underlying so many changes there are some
things which do not change and are ultimately
founded on Christ, who is the same yesterday,
today and for ever'.   GS 10

   This does not mean that we should not want
to express these universal moral norms in the
light of different cultural context, so that they
can be better understood and their relevance   Vinc Ler
can be more easily grasped. But the truth of   Comm 23
the law remains valid *'eodem sensu eademque*   PL 50,688
sententia' in its very substance and meaning.   DS 3020f

II. Conscience and Truth

Man's sanctuary

54   Man's conscience plays a fundamental role in
     relating his freedom to God's law. As Vatican
     II stated 'In the depths of his conscience man
     detects a law which he does not impose on
     himself, but which holds him to obedience.
     Always summoning him to love good and
     avoid evil, the voice of conscience can when
     necessary speak to his heart more specifically:
     "do this, shun that". For man has in his heart
     a law written by God. To obey it is the very
     dignity of man; according to it he will be
     judged' (Rom 2,14−16).   GS 16

     But we must understand what is the
     meaning of the moral conscience. If we set
     freedom and law in opposition we can exalt
     the former and produce a 'creative'
     understanding of conscience which diverges
     from the teaching of the Magisterium.

55   This leads some theologians to say that
     conscience provides general guidance and not
     a binding objective criterion. They stress the

complexity of psychological and emotional factors and the social and cultural environment. They also demand that the individual should make decisions not judgements and that these must be truly autonomous, so that moral maturity is attained, and that the position of the Magisterium inhibits such a process by its categorical stance.

56 This amounts to adopting a double standard of moral truth. On one side is the doctrinal, abstract truth and on the other the concrete circumstances. If we concentrate on the circumstances we can be permitted to commit what is intrinsically evil in good conscience. Thus 'pastoral' solutions contrary to the teaching of the Magisterium are justified ...

The judgement of conscience

57 St Paul says that conscience in a certain sense confronts man with the law: 'When Gentiles who have not the law do by nature what the law requires, they are a law unto themselves, even though they do not have the law. They show that what the law requires is written on their hearts, while their conscience also bears witness and their conflicting thoughts accuse or perhaps excuse them' (Rom 2,14–15). Conscience becomes a 'witness' of faithfulness or unfaithfulness with regard to the law which is known only to the person and hidden from everyone else. It is in this sanctuary that the person knows what is his own response to the voice of conscience, but also it is here that man listens to the voice of God.

58 St Bonaventure teaches that 'conscience is like God's herald and messenger; it does not

command things on its own authority, but commands them as coming from God's authority, like a herald when he proclaims the edict of the king. This is why conscience has binding force.' Conscience is thus the witness of God himself, whose voice and judgement reach into the depths of man's soul and call him *fortiter* and *suaviter* (strongly and sweetly) to obey.

In II Lib Sent. dist 39, a1,q.3.

59 But St Paul does not merely recognise conscience as a witness; he also analyses the way that conscience works. He speaks of conflicting thoughts which accuse or excuse the Gentiles in their behaviour (Rom 2,15). There is a judgement which either acquits or condemns according to whether such acts are in conformity or not with the law of God written on the heart. The author also speaks of the final judgement passed on such actions 'on that day when (according to the Gospel I preach), God will judge the secrets of men by Christ Jesus' (Rom 2,16).

The judgement of conscience is a practical judgement which applies to a concrete situation the rational conviction that one must love and do good and avoid evil. Whereas the natural law discloses the objective demands of morality, conscience applies the law to a particular case, formulating the moral obligation in the light of the natural law.　　CD 144

60 The judgement of conscience does not establish the law but rather bears witness to the authority of the natural law. Man must however act in accordance with it because such authority derives from the truth established by the divine law.

61 If someone does evil, the just judgement of his
conscience remains within him as a witness to
the universal truth of the good, as well as to
the malice of his particular choice. But the
verdict is a pledge of hope and mercy,
reminding him of the need to ask for
forgiveness while it bears witness to the evil
committed.

The practical judgement of conscience
which imposes an obligation, reveals the link
between freedom and truth. Far from
liberating conscience from objective truth,
one is truly free by searching for that truth and
being guided by it.

62 But conscience, considered as practical
judgement can be mistaken. This can be the
result of invincible ignorance, or through
one's own fault: 'When a man shows little
concern for seeking what is true and good, and
conscience becomes almost blind from being
accustomed to sin.' In cases of invincible   GS 16
ignorance the individual is not culpable and
even though conscience directs him to act in a
way that is not in conformity with objective
truth, it continues to speak in the name of that
truth. But there is a need to be aware of the
possibility of error: 'Do not be conformed to
this world but be transformed by the renewal
of your mind, that you may prove what is the   1 Tim 1,5
will of God, what is good and acceptable and   2 Tim 1,3
perfect' (Rom 12,2).   2 Cor 4,2

63 We must not confuse a 'subjective' error
about moral good with the 'objective' truth   Aquinas
proposed, or make the moral value of an act   De Veritas
performed with a correct conscience equiva-   Q. A. a.4
lent to the value of an act performed by
following the judgement of an erroneous
conscience because even though there may be

no culpability, it does not cease to be an evil and a disorder in relation to the truth, and so does not contribute to the perfection of the individual. For this reason the Psalmist prays: 'Who can discern his errors? From hidden faults acquit me' (Ps 18,12). Jesus also reminds us of the danger of allowing a blindness to envelop our judgement: 'The eye is the lamp of the body. So if your eye is sound, your whole body will be full of light; but if your eye is not sound, your whole body will be full of darkness. If then the light in you is darkness, how great is the darkness!' (Mt 6,22–23).

64 We are called by Christ to form our conscience, continually aligning it on what is true and good. It is not sufficient to be versed in the knowledge of God's law, there should be a certain oneness between man and the true good, which is developed by the practice of the virtues: 'He who does what is true comes to the light' (Jn 3,21). It is also assisted by the Magisterium of the Church. A pronouncement on moral questions does not undermine the freedom of conscience of Christians, because freedom is always 'in' the truth not 'from' the truth, and the Magisterium is not drawing attention to truths which are extraneous but rather pointing out what should already be possessed.

Aquinas ST II–II Q 44 a.2 DH 14

III. Fundamental Choice and Specific Kinds of Behaviour

'Only do not use your freedom as an opportunity for the flesh' (Gal 5,13)

65 Such is the interest in behavioural sciences that many point out how freedom is not only

the choice for one particular action but also within that choice, a decision about oneself, for or against the Good and ultimately for or against God.

This has developed in some authors into the theory of the fundamental option whereby the person does not exercise his choice on the conscious level, but rather in a transcendental way. Particular acts which flow from such an option would constitute only a partial expression and a sign or symptom of the choice. These particular 'goods' although in practice the way in which the fundamental option is expressed would not, in the opinion of some theologians, be capable of determining such an option. A distinction is thus introduced between the fundamental option and the deliberate choices of a concrete kind of behaviour. Some authors even limit moral 'good' and 'evil' to the dimension proper to the fundamental option. This leads to a two tier morality in which there is an order of good and evil dependent on the will; and specific kinds of behaviour in another order which are judged morally right or wrong according to calculations made concerning the 'pre-moral' or 'physical' goods and evils which actually result from the action.

66 Scripture acknowledges the importance of a fundamental choice 'by which man makes a total and free self-commitment to God, offering 'the full submission of intellect and will to God as he reveals'. Israel was called to accept The Commandments (cf. Jos 24, 14–25; Ex 19,3–8; Mic 6,8). In the New Covenant there is the fundamental call to follow Christ (cf. Mt 13,44–45;19,21). Such a vocation marks the greatest possible exaltation of human freedom while at the

DV 5
DS 3008

same time involves acts of faith and decisions which could be described as a fundamental option. But there is a danger that we can separate the fundamental option of an act of faith from particular choices: 'You were called to freedom, brethren. Only do not use your freedom as an opportunity for the flesh' (Gal 5,13).

67 By a fundamental choice man is capable of progressing towards perfection following the call of God. But this is actually exercised through conscious and free decisions of particular choices. It can also be revoked by conscious decisions to the contrary when dealing with grave matter. The morality of human acts are not determined only by one's intention, orientation or fundamental option without any corresponding effort to fulfil the obligations of the moral life. Every choice implies a will to pursue good or avoid evil in a particular context. In the case of behaviour which is branded as intrinsically evil there is no room for the 'creativity' of any contrary determination whatsoever.

68 The danger of this position can be seen when we consider the argument, that an individual, by virtue of a fundamental option could remain faithful to God independently of whether or not certain of his actions or choices are in conformity with specific moral norms. But man does not lose salvation simply by being unfaithful to a fundamental option. He also offends God, the giver of the law by every freely committed mortal sin: 'For whoever DV 5 PH 10 keeps the whole law but fails in one point has become guilty of all of it' (Jas 2,10). As the RP 17

Council of Trent teaches, 'the grace of justification once received is lost not only by apostasy, by which faith itself is lost, but also by any other mortal sin.'   DS 1544, 1569

Mortal and venial sin

69 A reflection on the fundamental option has also led some theologians to regard mortal sin which separates man from God as only the result of an act which engages the whole personality and on a level which is beyond any single act of choice. They would therefore argue that it is difficult to accept how mortal sins could be so easily and repeatedly committed or so easily repented. The gravity ought to be measured not by the *matter*, but rather by the degree of engagement involved.

70 The 1983 Synod of Bishops 'not only reaffirmed the teaching of the Council of Trent concerning the existence and nature of mortal and venial sins, but it also recalled that mortal sin is sin whose object is grave matter and which is also committed with full knowledge and deliberate consent.' Moral   RP 17 theology and pastoral practice has made us familiar with the case of an act which is grave, but does not constitute a mortal sin because of a lack of full awareness or deliberate consent on the part of the person committing it. But this should not be extended to make mortal sin an act of fundamental option: 'For mortal sin exists also when a person knowingly and willingly, for whatever reason, chooses something gravely disordered. In fact, such a choice already includes contempt for the divine law, a rejection of God's love for humanity and the whole of creation: the person turns away from God and loses charity. Consequently, the

fundamental orientation can be radically
changed by particular acts.' The separation of   RP 17
fundamental option from deliberate choices
of particular kinds of disordered and evil
behaviour which would not engage that option
effectively involves a denial of the Catholic
doctrine on mortal sin.

IV. The Moral Act

Teleology and teleologism

71 The relationship between man's freedom and   GS 17
the law of God is worked out in human moral   Greg.
acts. These do not merely change the state of   Nyss.
    De Vita
affairs extrinsic to man, but if they are   Moy
deliberate choices, define the person who   II,2–3
performs them: 'we are in a certain way our   PG
own parents, creating ourselves as we will, by   44,327–8
our decisions'.

72 The first question of the young man : 'What
good must I do to possess eternal life?' (Mt
19,6) brings out the essential connection
between the moral value of an act and man's
final end, his true good in whom he finds
perfect happiness. Only an act in conformity
with the good can be a path that leads to life.
    Morality is that rational ordering of the
human act to do good and the pursuit of that
good by the will. There must be that
conformity with the good and not simply an   Aquinas
intention on behalf of the subject or merely a   ST II–II
means to an end.   Q148 a.3

73 For the Christian the morality of his actions is
measured by that dignity and vocation which
have been bestowed on him by grace, making

him a new creation. 'Christ forms us', according to St Cyril of Alexandria 'in such a way that the traits of his divine nature shine forth in us through sanctification and justice and the life which is good, and in conformity with virtue ... The beauty of this image shines forth in us who are in Christ, when we show ourselves to be good in our works.' The Christian is called to order his acts to God, the supreme good and end (*telos*) of man which is safeguarded by observing the commandments (cf. Mt 19,17), so that he may appear before the judgement seat of Christ to give an account of his actions.

Tratatus ad Tiberium Diac. soc. II

2 Cor 5,10

74 When we consider the sources of morality, we have to ask whether the intention, the circumstances or the object determine the outcome. Certain ethical theories called *teleological* claim that criteria for evaluating the moral rightness of an action can be drawn from weighing the non-moral or pre-moral good to be gained and the corresponding non-moral or pre-moral values to be respected, and of maximizing or minimizing the evil. Many Catholic moralists who put forward this argument distance themselves from any utilitarian or pragmatic context.

75 But some do not take into consideration the fact that the will is involved in concrete choices which are a condition of its moral goodness; and others separate freedom from its actual determination through concrete kinds of behaviour. This can be called *consequentialism* or *proportionalism* depending on whether one calculates the consequences foreseeable or the proportion between the greater evil or the lesser good which arises in a particular situation.

These ethical theories while acknowledging
the insights of reason and revelation maintain
that there is no behaviour which can be pro-
hibited because it conflicts with certain moral
values. The values of a human act could be both
of the moral order (love of God, love of
neighbour, justice etc.,) and or the pre-moral
order (health, life, death, loss of property).
Moral goodness would therefore be judged both
on the basis of the intention in reference to the
moral order and its rightness on the basis of the
foreseeable effects or consequences. Concrete
kinds of behaviour could be judged 'right' or
'wrong' without it being possible to judge as
morally 'good' or 'bad' the will of the individual
choice. Thus behaviour which was considered
illicit according to traditional moral theology
would not be judged objectively evil, even
though contrary to the commandments.

76 Yet St Paul, summing up the fulfilment of the
law in the precept of love of neighbour as oneself
(Rom 13,8 – 10) reinforces the commandments
by revealing their requirements and their gravity.
Christians are called to accept even martyrdom
rather than perform any act which is contrary to
faith or virtue (cf. Acts 4,19;5,29).

77 It is of course necessary to consider the
intention and the *consequences* of any human
action. This was the basis of Jesus' dispute
with the scribes and Pharisees who paid lip
service to the outward observation while their
heart was elsewhere (Mk 7,20 – 21; Mt 15,19).
It is also necessary to consider the balance of
good and evil. But all these are insufficient to
judge the morality of a concrete choice. Such
calculations are always open to debate and
how can that serve as a reliable norm for a sure
morality?

78 The determination of the morality of a human act must depend on the *object* rationally chosen by a deliberate will. By object one does not mean a process or an event, but rather the objective of a deliberate decision which is willed by the individual. Thus, as the *Catechism of the Catholic Church* states 'there are certain specific kinds of behaviour that are always wrong to choose, because choosing them involves a disorder of the will, that is, a moral evil.' A moral act which is ordered to its ultimate good attains that good by being actually ordered to God in charity. Aquinas ST I–II Q18 a.6 CC 1761

'*Intrinsic evil*': it is not licit to do evil that good may come of it (Rom 3,8)

79 The primary and decisive element which enables one to judge the morality of a human act is the object ordered to the Good which is God.

80 Certain objects of the human act are by their nature incapable of being ordered to God and are always and *per se* (of themselves) intrinsically evil quite apart from ulterior intentions of the subject or the circumstances. Vatican II gives examples of these 'Whatever is hostile to life itself, such as any kind of homicide, genocide, abortion, euthanasia and voluntary suicide; whatever violates the integrity of the human person, such as mutilation, physical and mental torture and attempts to coerce the spirit; whatever is offensive to human dignity, such as subhuman living conditions, arbitrary imprisonment, deportation, slavery, prostitution and trafficking in women and children; degrading conditions of work which treat labourers as mere instruments of profit, and not as free RP 17

responsible persons'. This also pertains to the intrinsically evil acts of contraception because 'it is never lawful, even for the gravest reasons to do evil that good may come ... to intend directly something which of its very nature contradicts the moral law'.

GS 27

HV 14

81 If acts are intrinsically evil, a good intention or particular circumstances can diminish their evil, but not remove it: 'As for acts which are themselves sins like theft, fornication, blasphemy, who would dare affirm that, by doing them for good motives, they would no longer be sins, or, what is even more absurd, that they would be sins that are justified?' Circumstances or intentions can therefore never transform an intrinsically evil act into one that is subjectively good or defensible.

CC 1753f
Aug
Contra
Mend
7,18
PL 40,528

82 Acts whose object is not capable of being ordered to the Good are always and in every case in conflict with that good and cannot be otherwise.

83 The whole question of the existence of intrinsic evil in given human acts as taught by the Church comes from her understanding of man himself and the nature of truth. He can understand and live his vocation to freedom only in obedience to the commandments through the gift of the Holy Spirit.

CHAPTER THREE

'LEST THE CROSS OF CHRIST BE EMPTIED OF ITS POWER' (1Cor 1,17)

Moral Good for The Life of The Church and of The World

'For freedom Christ has set us free' (Gal 5,1)

84 The question of the relationship of man's freedom to God's law is ultimately that between freedom and the true good of man. Pilate's question: 'What is truth?' reflects the perplexity of the human person who no longer knows who he is, where he comes from, and where he is going to. This results in the descent into self-destruction, the contempt for human life, the violation of human rights and the wanton destruction of basic foodstuffs.

It is also the case that man is no longer convinced that only in the truth can he find salvation. This leaves freedom to decide for itself what is good and evil. In theology this leads to a lack of trust in the wisdom of God guiding man through the precepts of the moral law.

85 The Church cannot simply denounce or refute these ethical theories without helping all the faithful to form their consciences in accordance with the truth. It finds the answer to the Rom 12,2 problem of morality in the Crucified Christ who shows us the authentic meaning of freedom in the total gift of self : 'We preach Christ

50

crucified, a stumbling block to Jews and folly
to Gentiles, but to those who are called, both
Jews and Greeks, Christ the power of God and
the wisdom of God' (1 Cor 1,23 – 24).

86 Man has only to reflect on his own experience
to discover the extent of the limits of his own
freedom. Human freedom is given to us as a
gift, an essential part of our dignity as a
person called to the true Good and through
the revelation of Christ, to share the life of
God. At the same time this experience reveals
the capacity to reject the truth and for that
reason freedom itself needs to be set free by
Christ who alone comes to our rescue (Gal
5,1).

87 Christ reveals to us that the way to true
freedom lies in an open acceptance of the
truth: 'You will know the truth, and the truth
will set you free' (Jn 8,32). We are called to
worship him in spirit and truth (Jn 4,23),
because in this worship we become free. But
by contemplating Christ who gave himself up
for us even to the Cross, we understand that
freedom involves the gift of self out of love.
The Church, and each of her members is thus
called to share in this regal office (*munus
regale*) of the Crucified Christ who came 'not
to be served but to serve, and to give his life as   LG 36
a ransom for many' (Mt 20,28).   RH 21

Walking in the light (1 Jn 1,7)

88 It is imperative that Christians recognise the
destructive   consequence   of   separating
freedom from truth, which results in faith
being divorced from morality. It is through
our faith that we are able to judge the culture

in which we live, as St Paul reminds us 'Once
you were darkness, but now you are light in
the Lord; walk as children of the light (for the
fruit of the light is found in all that is good and
right and true), and try to learn what is
pleasing to the Lord. Take no part in the
unfruitful works of darkness, but instead
expose them' (Eph 5,8 – 12; cf. 1 Thes 5,4 – 8).
Faith is not simply a set of propositions to be
accepted by the intellect, but rather a lived
knowledge of Christ and a living remembrance of his commandments which enables
us to live as he lived in love of God and of our
brethren.

89 Faith lived becomes 'confession' before God
and in the sight of men because 'a city set on a
hill cannot be hid. Nor do men light a lamp
and put it under a bushel, but on a stand, and
it gives light to all in the house' (Mt 5,14 – 16).
Such witness expressed in the free gift of self
after the example of Christ can lead the
believer to martyrdom (Lk 9,23; Eph 5,1 – 2).

Martyrdom, the exaltation of the inviolable holiness of God's law

90 The relationship between faith and morality is
illustrated most strikingly in the respect due to
the personal dignity of every man which is
made manifest in the absolute prohibition of
actions which are intrinsically evil. The
unacceptability of 'teleological', 'consequen-
tialist' and 'proportionalist' ethical theories is
confirmed in the continuing witness of
Christian martyrdom.

91 We find such witness in the Old Testament for
example in the story of Susanna who chose

rather death than sin (Dan 13,22–23). At the dawn of the New Testament, John the Baptist spoke out on behalf of God's law and paid the supreme price. In the New Testament both the deacon Stephen and the apostle James died as martyrs in order to profess their faith and their love for Christ and they were followed by countless others who accepted persecution and death rather than betrayal and sin.

92 Martyrdom accepted as an affirmation of the inviolability of the moral order bears witness both to the holiness of God's law and the personal and inviolable dignity of man. It is a rejection of any false 'human' meaning one might attribute to an act which is intrinsically evil. Hence, St Ignatius of Antioch addressing the Christians of Rome says, 'Have mercy on me, brethren: do not hold me back from living ... Let me arrive at the pure light; once there *I will be truly a man.* Let me imitate the passion of my God'.

Ad Romanos 6,2–3 F X Funk I 260–1

93 Fidelity to the law of God, witnessed to by death is an outstanding sign of the holiness of the Church. The life of martyrs and, in general, all the Church's saints which is transfigured by the splendour of truth help to ward off any confusion in people's mind between good and evil and reawaken a moral sense by being a living reproof to those who transgress the law (cf. Wis 2,12; Is 5,20). Even though few are called to such a great sacrifice, all Christians are called with the grace of God to that sometimes heroic commitment by which one can actually 'love the difficulties of this world for the sake of eternal rewards'.

Gregory I Mor in Job 7,21,24 PL 75,778

94 But Christians are not alone in this. There is a moral sense present in all the great religious

and sapiential traditions of East and West. The words of the poet Juvenal apply to all: 'Consider it the greatest of crimes to prefer survival to honour and, out of love of physical life, to lose the very reason for living'. Satires 8,83–4

Universal and unchanging moral norms at the service of the person and of society

95 There are those who see the Church's teaching, especially when it draws attention to intrinsically evil acts, as intransigent and lacking compassion, in contrast to her role as Mother. But the Church's motherhood cannot be separated from her teaching mission: 'As Teacher, she never tires of proclaiming the moral norm ... The Church is in no way the author or the arbiter of this norm. In obedience to the truth which is Christ, whose image is reflected in the nature and dignity of the human person, the Church interprets the moral norm and proposes it to all people of good will, without concealing its demands of radicalness and perfection.' In FC 33 fact genuine compassion involves love for the true good of the person not concealing moral truth, but proposing it as a service to man, to the growth of his freedom and his ultimate happiness. This does not mean that she is not patient and rich in mercy towards sinners while being uncompromising towards the sin itself, with no exception of persons. HV 29

96 Only a morality which acknowledges certain norms as always valid can guarantee a valid foundation for society on the national and 97 international levels.

Morality and the renewal of social and political life

98 There is increasing indignation felt in the face of social and economic injustice and political corruption which holds human rights in contempt. This can only be corrected by a radical personal and social renewal based on the truth of God, the Creator and Redeemer, and the truth of man, created an redeemed by him.

99 Truth alone is capable of overcoming the various totalitarianisms that threaten our society. This, the Church presents in her social teaching and in her moral theology as well as in the *Catechism of the Catholic Church*.

CA 44
SRC 41

100 The Catechism draws attention both to temperance, justice and solidarity and proceeds to outline the kinds of behaviour and actions that are contrary to human dignity. It continues: 'The seventh commandment prohibits actions or enterprises which for any reason − selfish or ideological, commercial or totalitarian − lead to the enslavement of human beings, disregard for their personal dignity, buying, selling or exchanging them like merchandise. Reducing persons by violence to use-value or a source of profit, is a sin against their dignity as persons and their fundamental rights.'

2407−2413

2414

101 On the political level the transcendent value of the person and the objective moral demands of States, must underline truthfulness and openness in public administration, respect for the rights of political adversaries, impartiality and justice towards those accused, the honest use of public funds and the rejection of means to remain in office at any cost. With the fall of

CL 42

Marxism and other totalitarian systems there is a danger that ethical relativism may be taken up by democratic governments and in the absence of any ultimate truth to guide or direct political activity can degenerate into a new totalitarianism.

CA 46

Grace and obedience to God's law

102 Although even in the most difficult situations man must maintain that essential harmony between freedom and truth, he is frequently tempted to break it : 'I do not do what I want, but I do the very thing I hate ... I do not do the good I want, but the evil I do not want' (Rom 7, 15.19). The source of this struggle is the wish to determine one's own independence which began in the original *Fall* when man first sinned.

But temptations can be overcome, because God not only gives us the commandments, but also the possibility of keeping them, as we Sir 15,19f read in the Council of Trent: 'But no one, however much justified ... should employ that rash statement, forbidden by the Fathers under anathema, that the commandments of God are impossible of observance ... For God does not command the impossible, but in commanding he admonishes you to do what you can and to pray for what you cannot, and he gives his aid to enable you. His commandments are not burdensome (cf. 1 Jn 5,3); his yoke is easy and his burden light' (Mt 11,30). DS 1536

103 Man always has before him the spiritual gift of hope thanks to the help of divine grace which cooperates with his own freedom and which is the gift of our Redeemer, flowing from his pierced side (cf. Jn 19,34). Christ has set us free from the domination of our concupis-

cence, to realize the entire truth of our being.
If we sin, it is not because the redemption is
imperfect, but because we have not made use
of the grace which flows from it. So that it is
not an 'ideal', but the dignity which is held out
to us.

104 The mercy of God takes full account of
human weakness, but this does not mean we
should ever make our weakness the criterion
of morality, so that we can feel self-justified
without any need of mercy. Such an attitude
spreads doubt about the objectivity of the
moral law, and encourages the mistaken
illusion that the law can be observed without
the help of grace.   Lk 18,9–14

105 If we accept, like the tax collector in the
parable, the gap that there is between the law
and unaided human capacity, we are
prompted to ask for the grace we need (cf.
Rom 7,24–25).

Morality and new evangelization

106 Because of the modern decline or dulling; of
the moral sense, which is linked to a loss of
faith, there is need for a new evangelization;
107 a proclamation to society of the Gospel which
is always new. Such a proclamation involves
the presentation of morality in the new life to
be lived and the new way to be followed. It
must therefore be carried out not only as word
proclaimed, but also as word lived; particularly when it shows up the beauty of truth and
the liberating force of God's love in the
holiness of people's lives. The lives of the
saints, and above all, the Virgin Mother of
God provide the model, the strength and the

joy needed to live in accordance with God's commandments and the Beatitudes of the Gospel. The moral life of the Christian has the value of a 'spiritual worship' (Rom 12,1 cf. Phil 3,3) flowing from and nourished by that source of holiness which is found in the Sacraments.

108 At the heart of the new moral life proposed by the new evangelization, there is the Spirit of Christ, the principle and strength of the Church which bears witness in holiness of life.

The service of moral theologians

109 The whole Church has been called to share in the prophetic mission of Christ and so bear witness by a consensus in matters of faith and morals to the anointing received from the Spirit of truth. The vocation of the theologian in the Church is specifically at the service of the 'believing effort to understand the faith'. Theology can only flourish and develop, in and through, belonging to the Church.   LG 12   DVt 6

110 Moral theology reflects scientifically on the Gospel as the gift and commandment of new life 'which professes the truth in love' (Eph 4,15). It is the task of the Magisterium not only to intervene in matters of faith but also in the moral sphere. This includes teaching specific moral precepts which oblige in conscience as well as warning of the possibility of falling into error.

Moral theologians have the duty of instructing the faithful and especially seminarians about those commandments and practical norms authoritatively declared by the Church. They are called to understand the reasons underlying these teachings, to expound   CIC 252, 659 them and demonstrate the interconnection they have with each other and their relation with man's final end. They must also give example by their loyal assent to such teachings.

DS 3016

HV 28

111 Moral theologians working together with professors of Scripture and Dogma are called to draw attention to the response that man must give to the vocation given to him by God, which comes by means of his growth in love within the context of the Church. Moral theology cannot be reduced to a body of knowledge worked out in the context of the behavioural sciences, but has to be measured against the primordial question: 'What is good or evil?

112 What must be done to possess eternal life? Moral principles are not dependent upon the historical context in which they are discovered: nor are culturally conditioned because although such insights cannot be disregarded when looking to establish the average response, faith teaches that normality is itself conditioned and affected by sin. Only faith points to that 'beginning' (Mt 19,8) and proclaims God's mercy.

113 Moral teaching cannot simply be a free-for-all as in a representative democracy, because opposition and dissent is an attack on ecclesial communion and is in no way a legitimate expression of Christian freedom or the diversity of the gifts of the Spirit. The theologians must teach within the communion of faith safeguarded by the hierarchy.

DVt
11,32–39

Our own responsibilities as Pastors

114 Pastors and Bishops of the Church have the
    duty of teaching the faithful those things LG 25
    which lead them to God, just as the Lord Jesus
    did with the rich young man whom he invited
    to follow him in poverty, humility and love.
    Christ gives us the task of providing the same
    response. Christian moral teaching must be
    one of the chief areas in which we exercise our
    pastoral guidance.

115 This is the first time that the Magisterium of
    the Church has set out in detail the
    fundamental elements of this teaching with
    the principles necessary to apply in practical
    and cultural situations. I have briefly recalled
    the essential characteristics of freedom as well
    as the fundamental values connected with the
    dignity of the person and the truth of his
    human acts and have evaluated certain trends
    in moral theology today. I entrust to you the
    task of strengthening your brethren just as
    Christ entrusted Peter (Lk 22,32). It is
    important to stress for the good of society that
    the moral commandments are universally
    valid and immutable, especially those which
    prohibit intrinsically evil acts. Such
    unwavering demands are based upon God's
    infinitely merciful love (Lk 6,36) leading us to
    the perfection of life which is worthy of the
    children of God.

116 As bishops we have an obligation within our
    dioceses to see that this moral teaching is
    faithfully handed down (cf. 1 Tim 1,10) with
    the strength that comes from our communion
    in faith with Peter, and under Peter as
    successors of the apostles. We must have a

particular concern for Catholic institutions whether these are schools, universities, health-care facilities or counselling services. If these do not live up to the title 'Catholic' it should be withdrawn.

CIC 808

117 In the heart of every Christian, in the depths of each person, there is always an echo of that question which the young man asked of Jesus: 'Teacher, what good must I do to possess eternal life?' (Mt 19,16). The Church's reply contains the voice of Jesus Christ, the truth about good and evil. This gentle but challenging voice becomes light and life through the anointing which the Spirit gives. We should have confidence because as St Paul tells us 'our competence is from God, who has made us competent to be ministers of a new covenant, not in a written code but in the Spirit ... The Lord is the Spirit, and where the Spirit of the Lord is, there is freedom. And all of us, with unveiled faces, reflecting the glory of the Lord, are being changed into his likeness from one degree of glory to another; for this comes from the Lord, the Spirit' (2 Cor 3,5–6,17–18).

CONCLUSION

Mary, Mother of Mercy

118 Let us entrust ourselves to Mary, Mother of God and Mother of Mercy. She is Mother of Mercy because her Son was sent by the Father as the revelation of God's mercy (Jn 3,16–17; Mt 9,13). His mercy towards us is Redemption and reaches its fullness in the gift of the Spirit who bestows new life and demands that it be lived; making possible the miracle of the perfect accomplishment of the good. We are freed from the slavery of evil and given the ability to do what is good, noble, beautiful and pleasing to God.

119 Christian morality is not complicated, since it consists ultimately in the simplicity of the Gospel, the following of Christ in that communion which is the Church. St Augustine tells us; 'He who would live has a place to live, and has everything needed to live. Let him draw near, let him believe, let him become part of the body, that he may have life. Let him not shrink from the unity of the members.' This does not take away the fact that reality is complex but it allows us to see how distinctive authentic Christian morality is, while giving us the energy we need to carry it out. The Church's Magisterium has the task of expressing the whole breadth of what the following of Christ implies, without obscuring its moral demands or their consequences. The one who loves Christ keeps his commandments (Jn 14,15).

In Ioannis Tr 26,13 CCL 36,266

120 Mary is also Mother of Mercy because she
obtains for us the divine mercy, asking from
the Father together with Christ, forgiveness
for those who know not what they do (cf. Lk
23,34).

She is the model of the moral life because
she lived and exercised her freedom by giving
herself to God and accepting God's gift within
her womb. By accepting and pondering in her
heart events which she did not fully
understand, she became the model of all those
who hear the word of God and keep it (Lk
11,28). She invites us as she invited the
servants at the wedding feast of Cana to
accept the Wisdom of the Eternal Word (Jn
2,5).

Mary shares our human condition, but
being without sin she is able to have
compassion on human weakness. But she does
not permit sinful man to be deceived by those
who claim to love him by justifying his sin, for
this would empty the Cross of Christ of its
power. Only through the Cross and
Resurrection can man obtain peace for his
conscience and live completely for the praise
of his glory (Eph 1,12).

Given in Rome, at St Peter's, on 6 August,
Feast of the Transfiguration of the Lord, in
the year 1993, the fifteenth of my Pontificate.

Joannes Paulus Pp II

ABBREVIATIONS

Aquinas
In *Duo Praec*epta Caritatis et in Decem Legis Praecepta
*In Epist*ola *ad Rom*anos
*S*umma Theologica
*Au*gustine
*Contra Faust*um
*Contra Mend*acium
In Ioannis Evangelii *Tr*actatus
Bonaventure
*In II Lib*rum Sententiarum
CA Centesimus Annus
CC Catholic Catechism
CD Contra Doctrinam (on Situation Ethics) 2 February 1956
CIC Codex Iuris Canonici (Code of Canon Law)
CL Christifideles Laici
Cyril of Alexandria
*Tractatus ad Tiberium Diac*onum sociosque
DH Dignitatis Humanae
DS Denzinger Schönmetzer
DV Dei Verbum
DVi Donum Vitae 22 February 1987
DVt Donum Vitae (on Theologians) 24 May 1990
FC Familiaris Consortio
FD Fidei Depositum (Apostolic Constitution introducing the
Catechism)
*Greg*ory *Nyss*a
*De Vita Moys*is
*Greg*ory I
*Mor*alis in Job
GS Gaudium et Spes
HG Humani Generis
HV Humanae Vitae

*Ign*atius of *Ant*ioch
Irenaeus AH Adversus Haereses
Leo XIII
  *Libertas Praestan*tissimum, 20 June 1888
LG Lumen Gentium
J H Newman
  *Diff*iculties of Anglicans vol *II*
OT Optatam Totius
PP Populorum Progressio
PH Personae Humanae (Sexual ethics) 29 December 1975
RH Redemptor Hominis
RP Reconciliatio et Paenitentia
SRC Sollicitudo Rei Socialis
Trent Council of Trent
*Vinc*ent of *Ler*ins
  *Comm*onitorium Primum

GLOSSARY OF TERMS

Consequentialism
A theory which proposes that the morally right choice should be based upon a calculation which maximises the good consequences and/or minimizes the evil.

Fundamental moral choice or option
The name given by some to one's fundamental self-commitment to God which argues that such an orientation can remain in place in spite of concrete actions or choices which are contrary to specific moral norms, for example, the Ten Commandments.

Natural Law
The presence in creation of divine wisdom, which in man calls him to do good and to avoid evil.

Pre-moral goods and evils
The name given to certain events, especially those brought about by human choice, which according to some are to be included in an assessment of the morality of the choice one might make (cf. Consequentialism and Proportionalism). Thus a surgeon it is said, in choosing to amputate, is bringing about the (pre-moral) evil of depriving the patient of his leg. It is argued therefore that we may sometimes choose evil that good may come.

Proportionalism
A theory which proposes that the morally right choice is the one which will bring about a better proportion of benefit to harm than any other available choice.

Situation Ethics
A theory which argues that the morality of an action is to be determined by the total context in which it is to be performed and that the decisive details may not be understood by the application of specific moral norms.

Theonomy
God's wisdom and providence (literally *God's law*), in which man shares, by the free obedience of his reason and will.

INDEX

Individual references to *Jesus Christ, The Church* and *Vatican II* which occur throughout, are not provided for reasons of space.